Original title:
Camellia Confessions

Copyright © 2025 Creative Arts Management OÜ
All rights reserved.

Author: Natalia Harrington
ISBN HARDBACK: 978-1-80566-764-3
ISBN PAPERBACK: 978-1-80566-834-3

The Blooming Soul's Echo

In the garden where secrets play,
Petals gossip in a light ballet.
A flower sneezed, how rude, you see,
Blushing bright as it stood with glee.

With a wink, the daisies shared a joke,
'The roses are thorns, but we're no hoax!'
Laughter echoed, a sweet perfume,
As bees buzzed in, to join the boom.

A tulip twirled, wearing purple shades,
Claiming the sun in crafty charades.
"I'm the fairest, come look, don't miss!"
While the violets whispered, "What bliss!"

In this floral crowd, tales unfold,
Of bumbles and blunders, all brave and bold.
So join the fun in this sprightly dance,
Where blooms can giggle and often prance.

The Blossom's Silent Song

In the garden, blooms so bright,
Whispers of petals take to flight.
They gossip soft, beneath the sun,
About the bees and their sweet fun.

Dancing leaves in a breezy sway,
Laughing loudly at the stray.
The sunbeams tickle with delight,
While flowers share tales through the night.

Petals of Truth Unfurled

Gather 'round, oh fragrant bunch,
With secrets hidden, a playful hunch.
One petal screams, "I've got the scoop!"
Another giggles, "Join the group!"

A bloom confesses, it once did sway,
With a bumblebee, on a sunny day.
Petals blush, oh what a sight,
As they share laughter, pure and light.

Secrets Wrapped in Green

Under leaves where shadows play,
Secrets whisper, come what may.
A bug who thinks he's quite the spy,
Finds all the gossip passed on high.

Wrapped in green, the chitchat flows,
Of raindrops dancing on the toes.
Laughter echoes, while petals grin,
The chase for truth is where we begin.

Fragrant Longings

A bloom once dreamed of distant lands,
While swaying soft with gentle hands.
It longed for laughter, sweet and bold,
In stories shared and secrets told.

Petals sighed of zesty cheer,
Yearning for laughter, year after year.
As fragrances float on the breeze,
Together they dance, with perfect ease.

The Language of Secret Gardens

In whispers soft, the flowers talk,
Their petals giggle as the bees do walk.
Secrets shared beneath the moon,
A garden choir in floral tune.

With every bloom, a tale unfolds,
Of mischief done and dreams retold.
Their roots entwined in jest and glee,
In hidden plots, they plot with glee.

In the Shade of Blossoms

Here under branches, shadows play,
Dancing softly through the day.
Petals drop like jokes once told,
Each bloom a story, bright and bold.

The gardener laughs, what a sight!
Unruly blooms in comical flight.
Watch out for roses, they might bite,
A jest in every thorny plight.

The Confession of Petals

A sunflower grinned, seeds in a row,
"Who knew a bud could steal the show?"
The tulips nodded, feeling grand,
Confessions shared at nature's hand.

"Last night, I snuck into the vase!"
A petunia blushed with a cheeky grace.
They swayed and swirled, a giggling plot,
In the garden, laughter hit the spot.

Unraveled in Bloom

The daffodils danced in silly lines,
Exchanging jokes and cheeky signs.
"What's more fun than a springtime fling?"
"A bumblebee in a jumpy swing!"

Among the petals, secrets spread,
Ticklish laughter with colors red.
Who knew a garden had such a scene?
Unraveled petals weave through green.

Beneath the Blooms' Embrace

Underneath blooms, secrets stray,
Bees gossip 'bout the sunny day.
With petals soft and colors bright,
I swear they laugh by morning light.

A breeze sneezed pollen, oh what noise!
The flowers giggled, oh how they poise.
Each bloom declares its own own jest,
'Oh dear, who wore that gaudy dress?'

A little bud with an awful pout,
Shouted, 'Why's my stem so stout?'
Daisies snickered, 'Try yoga!'
The tulips winked, 'It's just for show, ha!'

So let us dance in petals' sway,
And laugh as blooms lead us astray.
In this garden, joy's the art,
We'll never take ourselves too smart!

The Language of Earthly Whispers

In a chat with roots so deep,
They shared tales over coffee steep.
Whispers echo through the green,
A drama unfolds, oh how it's seen!

The daisies roll their eyes in jest,
'What's with that flower in a vest?'
Lilies shout, 'Oh give it time!'
While violets snicker, 'His style's sublime.'

Toads croak out the latest scoop,
As crickets hum and ants all troop.
'Heard the roses throw a ball?'
'Can't even bloom, they trip and fall!'

So join the hum of nature's show,
With flowers in a gossipy flow.
From roots to tips, they weave a thread,
Of laughter that is lightly spread.

The Shadow of a Fading Petal

Once stood a petal loud and proud,
Now whispers of decay, not allowed.
'Time to shine!' the sunbeam beams,
But fading petals have other schemes.

'I'm vintage,' quipped the wilted shade,
'I've seen more than you, my dear parade!'
With a wink, he'd tip his hat,
'Been here longer than your silly chat.'

With every breeze, his stories fly,
Of flirty bees and clouds up high.
Oh, what tales the shadows weave,
Of petals lost, yet still believe!

'Life's a cycle, and oh so funny!'
He chuckled low, 'But sweet like honey.'
In fading hues, his laughter rings,
A wisdom only time can bring.

Symphony of Unraveled Dreams

In a garden where the daisies prance,
They sing of love, a strange romance.
With every note, a flower sways,
Conducting dreams in quirky ways.

The violets laughed as they took the lead,
'We'll show them all, just plant the seed!'
Under the moon's enchanting glow,
Every petal dances, putting on a show.

And as the stars twinkled bright,
Roses murmured, 'What a night!'
Their velvet voices float in tune,
A melody that makes hearts swoon.

The symphony swells, with giggles in the air,
Flowers unite in joyful flair.
In every color, every scheme,
They laugh together, living the dream.

Embers Beneath the Blossom

In the garden, whispers play,
Petals gossip night and day.
A bee with shades, oh what a sight,
Buzzing tales from left to right.

Worms in tuxedos dance in pairs,
Composting secrets with flair.
Frogs recite their love's mishaps,
While sprouts giggle, clasping laps.

The roses roll their eyes, you see,
While daisies snicker secretly.
Clovers try to steal the show,
But bees just laugh, "We rule the row!"

So come join this odd charade,
In a world where laughter's made.
Beneath each bloom, a jest awaits,
In nature's hilarious states.

Petals of a Forgotten Dream

In a vase, the petals sigh,
Turning dreams to marzipan pie.
The sunbeams wink, the shadows tease,
As flowers spy on bumblebee knees.

Each dew drop tells a joke at dawn,
While thorns roll eyes, slightly drawn.
A tulip's blush is quite the prank,
While daisies dive in lines of rank.

Forget-me-nots, so sweetly bold,
Spread rumors that never grow old.
The daisies bet their blooms on chance,
That petals turn to serve for dance.

So raise a glass, or maybe two,
To flowers' tales, both wild and true.
In this garden, laughter streams,
With every petal's forgotten dreams.

Garden of the Soul's Secrets

In the secret garden's glow,
Butterflies flaunt their wiggly show.
A hedgehog's sold his memoirs grand,
While roses blush on every hand.

Gossamer threads hold giggles tight,
While daisies dance with all their might.
An owl laughs, "I'm wise, you see!"
But it's the plants who get the tea.

Shrubs gossip over brewed chamomile,
Planning pranks that have some zeal.
Violets in gowns of deep surprise,
Pretend they're stars in costume guise.

With every rustle, laughter calls,
Echoing through the ivy walls.
In this garden, secrets bloom,
With every gleeful, fragrant plume.

In the Shade of Blooming Truth

Under blooms where secrets weave,
Jokes and laughter never leave.
A peony blushes: "What a mess!"
While vines confess their snug caress.

A pair of daisies argue loud,
"Your jokes? They're just not allowed!"
But then they giggle, snickering low,
As a squirrel takes an acorn throw.

The lilacs serenade the bees,
With silly songs that sway the leaves.
Glorious petals flutter and tease,
In this shade, hearts dance with ease.

So gather 'round for tales and jest,
With every bloom, we're truly blessed.
In this shade, we find our roots,
And laughter grows in flowered suits.

Truths woven in Green

In the garden, gossips fly,
Petals whisper with a sigh.
Leafy secrets, oh so bold,
Told by blooms, never old.

Morning dew sees all the jest,
As bees buzz, they know the best.
Colors clash and laughter rings,
Nature's choir, joy it brings.

The vines twist tales of delight,
Frogs croak out the dead of night.
Sunlight dances through the leaves,
Even the soil chuckles, believes.

With every bud, a story grows,
In laughter's shade, the garden glows.
Sprouting truths, oh what a scene,
Under the watch of vibrant green.

Heartstrings among the Buds

Buds all nestled, cozy tight,
Strumming tunes in morning light.
Daisies wink, a playful tease,
Sunflowers sway with blissful ease.

Amidst the blooms, a date was set,
A bumblebee lost in a fret.
Can't decide which flower's best,
Each one's heart's a little jest.

Whispers shared between the stalks,
Nature's gossip—oh, it rocks!
Roses blush, while thorns just sigh,
In gardens where loves never die.

With each glow and fragrance sweet,
The garden turns to a love seat.
Woven hearts in petals round,
Where laughter and affection's found.

The Silent Resonance of Flora

In the hush of morning's grace,
Blooms have secrets, hidden space.
Chirping birds, they tune their song,
While daisies giggle all day long.

Whispers float on softest breeze,
A shy flower playing tease.
Petals blush, and so they sway,
Nature keeps the jokes at bay.

Garden gnomes, with knowing stares,
Watch the dance without a care.
Every leaf has tales to share,
As laughter fills the fragrant air.

In silence, blooms ignite their cheer,
For every laugh, they shed a tear.
Nature's whimsy paints the scene,
Where silence sings and life is green.

Veins of the Garden

Roots entwined in playful chase,
Worms decide to win the race.
Underneath, they giggle too,
In this soil, there's always crew.

Vines with jokes, a twist of fate,
Leaves declare they'd gamble late.
Every petal drips with glee,
While daisies sip their herbal tea.

With every bloom, the stories weave,
Of heart-shaped leaves that love to deceive.
Nature's humor, sly and sweet,
In this garden, life's a treat.

As twilight casts its glow so bright,
Flowers sway, bidding goodnight.
In the veins, the fun flows free,
With laughter echoing endlessly.

In the Heart of Wild Petals

In the garden, laughter blooms,
A bee's dance, a flower's tunes,
With petals bright, a cheeky grin,
Who knew plants could have such fun within?

Sunlight spills like spilled tea,
A bumblebee steals my scone with glee,
The roses whisper, 'Come and see!'
Oh, the petals have secrets, wild and free!

Chasing butterflies, I trip and fall,
The daisies giggle, I hear them all,
A marigold winks, it's quite the sprawl,
In this riotous garden, I'm having a ball!

Amongst the blooms, a tangle of laughs,
Comparing scents like a daring giraffes,
Petals chatter in hilarity's drafts,
Who knew wildflowers could write such drafts?

Beneath the Canopy of Secrets

Underneath the leafy shade,
The flowers share a serenade,
A rose blushes, 'I'm feeling grand!'
While daisies whisper, 'Take my hand.'

Violets giggle, 'What's your name?'
While tulips boast of garden fame,
The secrets flutter like a nightingale,
In this leafy realm, we all convail!

One sly daffodil starts to tease,
'Who's the fairest among us, please?'
Laughing petals playfully scheme,
In this floral hushed, we dream a dream!

A slumbering sunflower yawns with flair,
'I napped too long, but I'm still rare!'
The vines eavesdrop from up so high,
Oh, the laughter floats up to the sky!

The Language of the Hidden Heart

A tulip speaks in whispers soft,
Stirring stories from aloft,
Petals arch like giggling kids,
Who knew flowers hid such fibs?

Lilies chuckle, 'Do you feel that beat?'
With every sway, they dance on their feet,
In this hidden heart, laughter flows,
As secrets slip from bloom to rose.

'What's the gossip?' a daisy pries,
'Who loves whom, and all the lies?'
Pansies wink, with colors bright,
In this garden of jest, we ignite!

Hushed blooms trade their tales at dusk,
While a foxglove laughs—oh, what a musk!
Beneath moonlight, they spin delight,
In this flowery fun, all feels right!

Floral Fantasies and Fables

In a garden where dreams collide,
Petals swirl on a breezy ride,
With sequined wings, they hop and skip,
Oh, how flowers love a good quip!

A daisy dreams of castles high,
While sunflowers point to the sky,
Violet fairies twirl and spin,
'Let the floral fun begin!'

At twilight's glow, a rose comes forth,
'Tell me tales of merriment's worth!'
And the herbs around sigh in delight,
As crickets join in, dancing in the night.

Petals plot in rhymes and riddles,
Playing games with soft giggles,
Under stars, a celebration grows,
In this whimsical world, anything goes!

An Unfurling of Secrets

In the garden of giggles, blossoms sway,
They whisper wild tales of a sunny day.
A bee with a bowtie buzzes with cheer,
While petals collude to spread laughter here.

The daffodils dance, their secrets exposed,
While squirrels plot mischief, they are the pros.
A gnome grins wide, with algae-green hands,
As blooms conspire to make zany plans.

Beneath leafy whispers, laughter erupts,
With dandelions sharing their wild hiccups.
The morning dew sprinkles in fits of delight,
As flora and fauna join in the plight.

In this patch of frolic, no room for gloom,
Each leaf and each stem creates joy to bloom.
With roots twisting stories, oh what a show,
In the garden of secrets, life's a grand flow.

Whispers of Petals

Petals are gossipers, oh what a sight,
They giggle and natter from morning to night.
A rose shares a tale of a handsome bee,
While tulips wink softly, just wait and see.

The daisies debate who's the fairest by far,
While violets chuckle, they've raised the bar.
In floral attire, with colors that clash,
They plot and they scheme for a glorious bash.

Bringing together the quirkiest crew,
With laughter and joy, it's a colorful view.
In the soft rustling breeze, they can't keep a vow,
Secretive petals can't help but avow.

So when you're wandering through gardens anew,
Listen closely, they're chatting just for you.
For in every whisper, lie stories untold,
In the heart of the blooms, there's laughter to hold.

Secrets in Bloom

In a world all a-buzz with the gossip of greens,
The flowers exchange their delightfully wild scenes.
A petunia blushes, sharing a crush,
On a handsome sunflower, oh, feel the rush!

Chatter of leaves, with each rustle and sway,
As secrets unfold in a whimsical way.
The lilacs conspire, spread rumors you bet,
While frogs in the bayou regret what they've met.

A lilting laughter, the breeze carries far,
As flora reminisce by the light of the star.
With roots intertwined in a playful embrace,
These secrets in bloom find their own little space.

And as night falls, they giggle and play,
Under moonlit splendor, they frolic away.
So come join the party in this floral jest,
For every bright petal knows how to fest.

A Garden of Heartstrings

In the heart of the garden, where laughter is found,
With cherry blossoms dancing, joy is unbound.
The sunflowers gossip of bees on the prowl,
While tulips roll their eyes at a daring old owl.

Among fragrant petals, the secrets take flight,
Each bloom sporting tales that tickle with light.
With whispers of wonder from roots that connect,
They share with the world a playful respect.

A patchwork of colors, giggles abound,
Each leaf has a story, a joy to confound.
The daisies form circles, spinning a yarn,
While violets and roses raise a toast with charm.

So wander this garden of heartstrings and fun,
Where laughter and secrets together are spun.
With blooms all a-twinkle, a party unfolds,
Where every petal's laughter will never grow old.

Unseen Garden Whispers

In a garden where secrets play,
Petals gossip, come what may.
Butterflies waltz with a grin,
Planting whispers in the wind.

Roses tease the shy daffodils,
Leafy friends sharing silly thrills.
Bumblebees buzz with a knowing glance,
While the tulips join in the dance.

The daisies wink with cheeky flair,
Mimicking the breezes in the air.
In this realm of leafy glee,
Nature's jesters hide with me.

So when you stroll through greens so bright,
Listen closely, laugh with delight.
For in this patch of quiet fun,
The flowers bloom, each one a pun.

Blooming Shadows

In the twilight, shadows bloom,
With giggles that dispel the gloom.
Laughter echoes among the leaves,
As the night gently weaves.

Petals prance in silver light,
Joking 'bout the day and its plight.
The moonlight teases every flower,
Making blooms chuckle hour by hour.

The bushes quip with gentle sass,
While the daisies nod, none should pass.
In this garden where jokes take flight,
Every bud hides a laugh tonight.

So when the sun begins to hide,
Join the blooms on this wild ride.
For even in shadows, fun can thrive,
Blooming smiles keep the night alive.

The Quiet Chorus of Flora

Amidst the greens, a chorus stirs,
Flowers sing as joy occurs.
Humor wrapped in silky vines,
Nature's jest in soft designs.

Ferns sway with a comical beat,
While petals gather, in sync they meet.
Lilies laugh in graceful pose,
A symphony of scents—who knows?

The sunflowers boast with prideful flair,
Started the chatter without a care.
Every leaf joins the playful song,
Nature knows where giggles belong.

So, if you wander, don't just glance,
Join the chorus, take a chance.
For in this garden, fun's the theme,
Let laughter reign, let joy beam!

The Dance of Hidden Thoughts

In the stillness, thoughts take flight,
Hidden dances ignite the night.
Roses twist with playful sway,
While whispers frolic, come what may.

The daisies plot a clever scheme,
With every breeze, they share a dream.
Tulips scribble tales in rhyme,
Sipping nectar, one sip at a time.

Thoughts pirouette on dewy blades,
In this realm where laughter invades.
Vines entwined, they spin around,
Creating joy in every sound.

So in this garden where thoughts roam free,
Tap your toes to their symphony.
Join the dance, spin with delight,
For hidden thoughts bring joy each night.

Whispers of the Bloom

In the garden, petals play,
Gossiping in the light of day.
They sneak around with cheeky flair,
Noses twitching in the air.

A daisy winks at a passing bee,
"Did you hear what Rose said to me?"
The tulips giggle, a riotous bunch,
Even violets munch at the lunch.

Winds carry secrets, swift and bold,
Petals whispering tales untold.
Each flower dons a playful mask,
In their blooming world, they dare to bask.

So next time you stroll in the sun,
Listen closely, have some fun!
The blooms know secrets, oh so sweet,
In the laughter, let your heart beat.

Secrets in Silk Petals

In silken folds, secrets hide,
Like a kitten who won't abide.
Petals rustle with cheeky glee,
Each one more clever than you and me.

A flower plays a game of charades,
Acting like it's in the parades.
With laughter hidden in each hue,
They spill the beans, a wild crew.

Roses whisper, 'Did you see?',
"Daffodil danced madly with a bee!"
Sunflowers nod with a knowing glance,
"Haven't seen that kind of romance!"

Amidst the bloom, the humor lies,
In fragrant scents, no need for disguise.
With every petal, a chuckle shared,
In this garden, nobody's scared.

The Language of Blossoms

Blossoms gossip in the breeze,
Sharing tales with utmost ease.
They wave their petals in delight,
   Chasing butterflies in flight.

Every flower knows their game,
"Watch that git, he's always late!"
Tulips giggle, daisies chime,
Beauty mixed with perfect rhyme.

Secret meanings in their hues,
A joke or two they always choose.
Under moonlit skies so bright,
They laugh and tease till morning light.

So if you wander through their zone,
Join the laughter, don't stay alone.
In the garden, humor flows,
With every bud, a smile grows.

Garden of Secrets

In a garden where laughter sings,
A parrot tells of flower flings.
Petals giggle, leaves give chase,
All day long, a playful race.

The peonies swirl, putting on a show,
"Can you believe what the marigolds know?"
Lilies nod, their heads held high,
"Just wait until you see them fly!"

Behind a bush, a sly rose peeks,
Spilling secrets of the week.
"What are you hiding?" asks the pine,
"Oh, nothing much, just a love divine!"

So join the dance among the blooms,
Where laughter echoes, and joy consumes.
In this garden, secrets blend,
With playful hearts that never end.

Whispers Across the Green

In the garden, secrets play,
Where flowers giggle through the day.
Roses blush at silly jokes,
While daisies dance in leafy cloaks.

Every petal has a tale,
Of bees in rapture, soft and frail.
Laughter drips from morning dew,
As sunbeams wink—a playful crew.

The grass tickles exposed toes,
While butterflies steal the show.
A rabbit snickers, hops, and prances,
As tulips share their wild glances.

With breezes swirling, laughter grows,
In leafy realms where fun bestows.
The garden's chorus, light and free,
Whispers joy, just wait and see.

The Melodies of the Unvoiced

In shadows quiet, whispers hum,
A melody of absent scum.
Plants know secrets we can't hear,
They chuckle softly, never fear.

A cactus shares a prickly grin,
While ferns debate who'll wear the pin.
The jolly moss knows all the fun,
As it rolls around in afternoon sun.

An oak tree sways with hearty jest,
In leafy laughter, it feels blessed.
Each branch a stage for merry skits,
As squirrels engage in comic fits.

In quiet corners, humor brews,
Among the petals, laughter snooze.
Nature's symphony, soft and bright,
Plays jokes unseen, with pure delight.

Threads of Nature's Lies

A spider weaves a tale so grand,
Daring bugs to take a stand.
"Catch me if you can!" they tease,
As they dodge with agile ease.

The roses boast their fragrant scent,
While violets plot a big event.
"Let's fool the bees," the tulips say,
"Let's trick them into going astray!"

Charming daisies wink with glee,
Kidding queens with false decree.
"Hear ye, hear ye," they proclaim,
"Flowers only! We'll play the name game!"

In this wild garden, fun transpires,
With flowery laughter and playful fires.
Nature's mischief, every day reveals,
The secrets draped in leafy feels.

The Blossom's Silent Scream

Petals croon in colors bright,
While blooms hide in cloaks of night.
They giggle softly, oh so sly,
As they watch the world pass by.

With whispers sweet, the buds conspire,
To outwit the sun's fierce fire.
"Let's play dead!" the orchids shout,
As they wiggle, twisting about.

A lilac laughs, a silent plea,
"When will they notice little me?"
So shy yet bold, with cheeks aglow,
In bloom's disguise, they steal the show.

Hence the garden giggles bright,
With giggling petals in moonlight.
In every flower, a story's spun,
A silent scream turned to silly fun.

Petal Conversations

In the garden, petals speak,
Whispers of secrets, oh so sleek.
One says, "I'm a flower on a diet!"
Another replies, "Oh, let's try a riot!"

Buds giggle at the bees that zoom,
Daring them to start a floral bloom.
"I'll wear a hat made of dew and lace!"
"I'd rather just roll in this sunny place!"

When the breeze comes, petals dance,
"Who knew pollen held such romance?"
One prances out, full of sass,
"I'll make all the other flowers pass!"

In the end, they're a silly crowd,
Bickering soft but still quite loud.
Who cares for thorns when smiles are bright?
We laugh till dusk, what a floral sight!

Through the Eyes of a Bloom

A rose rolled over and gave a sigh,
"Why do daisies always act so spry?"
A tulip grinned, "They think they're the stars,
But they barely know just who we are!"

With laughter soft as morning dew,
They plotted to paint the garden anew.
"Let's dress in colors that make them stare!"
"Or start a fashion—floral underwear!"

The sun chuckled as petals conspired,
While others watched, amazed and tired.
"What's next? A ball in the moonlight's glow?"
"Count me in! I'll wear my finest show!"

So blooms danced under the twilight sky,
Creating tales that made the stars sigh.
With petals like confetti, oh what a scene,
Laughter echoed where flowers convene!

Stories of the Flower's Heart

In the meadow, a marigold sighed,
"It's hard to bloom when you're so shy!"
The lavender laughed, her scent was sweet,
"Just flaunt your colors, feel the heat!"

A sunflowers' gossip rumbled around,
"Did you hear? The violets are quite profound!"
They claim to know all the secret trends,
But really, they just sit and pretend!

Roses rolled their eyes, with petals so bright,
"At least we know how to party all night!"
Whispers of love filled the balmy air,
While tulips giggled, lacking a care.

But beneath all the laughter, the truth did glow,
Every flower has tales, don't you know?
In their hearts are stories—each petal a page,
Creating a saga on nature's grand stage!

Mysteries of the Teardrop Flower

Once there was a flower with a tear,
"Why so sad?" asked the poppies near.
"I'm just reflecting on life's little mess,
Each drip's a story, I must confess!"

The daisies giggled, "Don't be so glum!
Your petals are pretty, and we're having fun!"
But the tearflower sighed, "You don't understand,
These drops hold the dreams I never planned!"

A bee buzzed in, with wisdom to share,
"Every petal's colored by the love in the air!"
"Tears add a sparkle, a twist to your tale,
Like rain on a road that makes flowers hail!"

So together they laughed under sunlit skies,
Transforming the teardrops into joyful cries.
For what is a flower if not a true friend,
With stories to tell that never quite end!

The Enigma of Blooming Hearts

In a garden filled with secrets,
Petals whisper lies so sweet.
A bee in love with blooms so bright,
Forgets to share his honey treat.

Daisies giggle, roses blush,
A two-faced fern starts to fuss.
Who knew flora could be sly?
Nature's gossip makes us sigh.

Butterflies dance, a waltz they learn,
While tulips turn and toss and churn.
With every swirl and every spin,
Garden drama's sure to win.

So let us toast with cups of dew,
To silly blooms that play peek-a-boo!
As petals prance, all for show,
The enigma of love will grow.

Veils of Botanical Whimsy

In this plot of leafy caps,
A basil plant dons fancy wraps.
It sneezes softly, to my delight,
"Excuse me!" it says, a funny sight.

Lilies giggle in the breeze,
Sharing jokes with bumblebees.
Petunias plan a masquerade,
In this garden, mischief's laid.

A cactus with a prickly grin,
Claims it's always sunbathing in.
But when the clouds pour out their tears,
It sheds its prickles, hides its fears.

In this realm of greens and games,
Each flower plays with silly names.
With every bloom a laughter's spun,
The whimsical dance has just begun.

When Leaves Cry

One rainy day, a leaf did weep,
Said, "Why must the sky be so deep?"
It called out to the nearest tree,
"Stop shaking, you're embarrassing me!"

The trees all laughed, a rustling choir,
"Don't worry, friend, we're all on fire!"
But when the sun peeked through the fog,
The leaf just shone like a happy dog.

A flower nearby tried to console,
"It's just a shower, don't lose control!"
And when the sunbeams cleared the skies,
Their laughter echoed, timeless sighs.

So when the leaves begin to moan,
Just know they're never all alone.
For every tear has silver lining,
In nature's tale, joy is defining.

The Poetry of Fragrant Memories

In the breeze, a whiff comes near,
Of blossoms laughing, full of cheer.
Jasmine spills tales from its bloom,
While minty whispers fill the room.

"Oh, do you recall that sunny day?"
Roses reminisce in a flowery ballet.
With every fragrance, tales unfold,
Of garden parties, bright and bold.

The lilac dreams of dances past,
While sunflowers gossip about the forecast.
With every scent, a giggle shared,
In fragrant memories, none were spared.

So here's a toast to blooms so bright,
Who weave our worlds in pure delight.
Each petal holds a laugh, a sigh,
In fragrant moments, we too fly.

Blooming Truths

In a garden of whispers, secrets swell,
Petals giggle softly, oh what a tell!
Each bloom has its quirks, a story to share,
Watch out for the thorns, they're quite debonair.

Sunlight beams down, the daisies conspire,
With tulips on jokes that never expire.
The roses are blushing, they know the game,
While lilies peek out, they're feeling the fame.

Secrets like pollen, they drift on the breeze,
Hiding in laughter among the tall trees.
No one can resist such colorful tales,
Garden gossip spreads like the wildest gales.

So come join the chatter, the blooms all unite,
In fragrant confessions that feel just right.
With petals and laughter, we'll share and we'll sing,
In this circus of blossoms, let the fun take wing.

A Tapestry of Petals

We weave our stories in colors so bright,
Each petal a tale in the soft morning light.
A daffodil trips, causing laughter to flare,
While violets chuckle, without a care.

Oh, the daisies dance, in a silly parade,
With tulip toe shoes that can't help but cascade.
Roses trade gossip, they snicker and tease,
While sunflowers stand high, feeling a breeze.

A tapestry spun, from giggles and grins,
The garden's a stage where the fun never thins.
Petals like actors in comedic delight,
Under the watch of the moon's gentle light.

So gather your blooms, let's share a good laugh,
In this whimsical garden, we'll write our own path.
With stories embroidered, we'll cherish the fun,
As petals keep spinning, all day 'til we're done.

The Shade of Vulnerability

In the soft, leafy shade where the petals find rest,
The blooms dare to share, feeling truly blessed.
With laughter like raindrops, they spill their sweet fears,
Sharing their secrets in the midst of cheers.

A shy little bud, with a soft, nervous laugh,
Talks of getting lost on its grand blooming path.
The others all chuckle, "We've been there too!"
In a circle of petals, there's comfort to view.

Sunlight and shadows play hide and seek,
Sharing their tales, the flowers feel unique.
Under the whispers, they find their own grace,
In the shade of the garden, they embrace their place.

So let's shed the armor, let's be brave and bold,
In this floral confessional, our stories unfold.
With giggles and blushes, we lighten the load,
In the shade of vulnerability, we've all found our road.

Revelations Among Roses

Amidst the roses, a ruckus ensues,
Petals proclaim truths while sipping on dew.
Each blossom reveals its most silly delight,
With blooms sharing jokes 'til the fall of the night.

The roses discuss all their mishaps and dreams,
Caught in the tangle of laughter and beams.
"Oh darling," says one, "I tripped over a bee!"
The petals all flutter, "You say that to me?"

With secrets exchanged, they giggle and sigh,
In the tapestry sweet, relationships fly.
They twist and they sway in the warm evening air,
Under moonlight's glow, there's joy everywhere.

So come join the frolic, the whispers will flow,
In gardens of laughter, come witness the show.
With roses so regal, we share and we dream,
In the realm of the blooms, we are all part of the team.

Beneath the Velvet Leaves

Beneath the velvet leaves they hide,
Where secrets blossom, and giggles abide.
A squirrel in a hat, all dapper and spry,
Whispers sweet nothings, then scurries on by.

In the garden, the gnomes start to dance,
With moves so silly, they take a chance.
A bumblebee winks, quite suave, I must say,
As it flirts with the daisies at the break of day.

Beneath the blooms, mischief is found,
With petals as pillows, they tumble around.
"Did you steal my sunshine?" a rose loudly shouts,
"Only borrowed it, darling! There's no need for doubts!"

In every corner, laughter's a treat,
With blossoms conspiring in the summer heat.
The ferns join the fun, their fronds all aglow,
As petals spill stories that only they know.

Petal Promises

With petals about, we craft our sweet dreams,
A joke from a lily, or so it seems.
"I'm blooming for fame," shouts the daffodil crew,
While snickering softly at the shy morning dew.

Promises made in the shade of green vines,
While daisies and sunflowers sip on sweet wines.
"Your fragrance is lovely! We'll call it a date!"
But the tulips just giggle, "Oh, isn't it great?"

The violets whisper, "Shush! Don't be loud!"
As a caterpillar joins, feeling quite proud.
He twirls through the petals, a charming display,
While everyone chuckles, then bursts into play.

Petal promises flutter like butterflies bright,
In the garden of laughter, where all feels just right.
An orchestra of chirps and rustling leaves,
Bring joy to the blooms and a giggle that weaves.

The Veil of Floral Thoughts

Behind a veil of blooms they convene,
With thoughts so silly, they craft a routine.
A poppy proposes they start a parade,
While hyacinths giggle, not wanting to fade.

"Oh, look at that blossom! It's wearing a crown!"
It's a daisy in disguise, feeling quite round.
The roses all blush, thinking such things,
As they scheme and they plot to show off their blings.

In the quiet of night, when stars start to twinkle,
A gladiolus sneezes and sets off a crinkle.
Petals fly high as they all breathe a sigh,
This flowered veil of thoughts, oh my, oh my!

With scents of laughter that dance through the air,
The blooms share their mischief, they truly don't care.
In this garden of whims, where humor runs free,
Their veil of floral thoughts is a sight full of glee.

Moonlit Murmurs

Under the moon, with giggles so light,
A daffodil whispers, "I'm quite a soft sight!"
The night blooms respond with a chorus of cheer,
As the crickets play on, their music so clear.

"Have you heard the news from the tulip so bold?"
She's painted her petals in lavender gold!
The violets clap, their applause like a spa,
While the peonies swoon, saying, "Oh, la la!"

With moths fluttering close, they join in the fun,
As they twirl to the rhythm, the night's just begun.
"Careful, don't trip on the dew!" one flower yells,
"Last time, it rained petals, and oh how it smells!"

Yet merriment lingers, as petals take flight,
In whispers of laughter that echo through night.
Moonlit murmurs weave tales of delight,
In this garden of whimsy, where joy takes its flight.

Petals Entwined in Truth

In a garden of lies, blooms unfold,
Whispers of petals, secrets untold.
A bee flew past, wearing shades of gold,
Sipping on gossip, it's quite bold.

Roses roll their eyes, oh what a scene,
While tulips giggle, oh so serene.
'Keep it hush,' says a shy daisy queen,
As plants tell tales, both funny and keen.

Reflections in Dewdrops

Morning dew drops, like little spies,
Catch all the gossip, it's no surprise.
Grass blades gossip with a wink and a sigh,
Tall tales pop up, reaching the sky.

A daffodil swoons at a snail's sweet tune,
While wisteria dances, floating like a balloon.
Laughter erupts beneath the bright moon,
In this floral fiesta, no room for gloom.

The Verses of Nature's Heart

Nature's heart beats with crickets' cheer,
Squirrels share jokes about acorns near.
Every leaf rustles, 'Can you hear?'
Spreading laughter, oh so dear.

Petals recite in a hilarious flow,
'Why did the bee start a dance show?'
The garden erupts with its own glowy glow,
As flowers recount stories, stealing the show.

Secrets Held in Green

Under the ferns, secrets take flight,
A grasshopper texts, 'You up for a fight?'
While daisies snicker, with petals so bright,
Nature's comedy club, all feels just right.

Leaves chime in with a rustling laugh,
'What's a tree's favorite math?
Branching out, never a gaffe!'
In this green delight, we're all on the path.

Echoing in the Garden

In the garden where whispers grow,
Flowers giggle, putting on a show.
They trade secrets with the busy bees,
And laugh aloud in the playful breeze.

The daisies roll and the roses blush,
While tulips tango in a colorful hush.
The sun sneaks peeks in a golden way,
As plants plot mischief day by day.

There's gossip 'bout the morning dew,
Chit-chat shared between green and blue.
A ladybug winks, taking a ride,
On the back of a snail with worms for pride.

When the moon lets laughter out at night,
Stars join in, twinkling with delight.
In this garden where joy abounds,
Funny tales are flourishing all around.

Touched by Petal's Grace

Do petals blush or simply glow?
When the gardener trips, oh what a show!
They wave goodbye, then gently fall,
Landing right on his hat—what a brawl!

The daisies gossip about the sun,
While orchids think they're oh-so-fun.
Near a lily, a frog leaps high,
Creating ripples, oh my, oh my!

A bee in a tux buzzes with flair,
Trying to impress a sweet summer air.
But when he trips on a clover's tip,
Stumbles and tumbles; oh, what a blip!

Yet in this realm of constant giggles,
Nature dances, it winks and wiggles.
Every flower knows when joy's in breach,
Their humor, a lesson, is what they teach.

Nature's Untold Stories

Under the boughs, tales begin to bloom,
With crickets chirping, they fill the room.
The wind carries whispers, meandering sly,
As butterflies argue, "I'm prettier, oh my!"

A squirrel in shades, wearing a hat,
Hiding a stash of snacks in a gnat.
He thinks he's clever with his nutty ploy,
While a crow plots to steal his prized joy!

The sprinkle of raindrops starts a new scene,
The flowers dance, all dressed in green.
They twirl and spin in a watery round,
Making the grass laugh with a joyful sound.

Bold bark from a tree, wisdom gone wild,
Tales of the forest, as laughter piled.
It's nature's own comedy, lush and bright,
Where surprises await in the soft daylight.

Secrets of the New Blossoms

The buds hold secrets, some cheeky, some bold,
While blooms burst forth in a tale to unfold.
They chatter and giggle in early light,
Swapping stories, both silly and bright.

A bumblebee strolls in, lacking all grace,
Stumbling on petals, joining the race.
"Excuse me!" he grins, with his fuzzy charm,
Falling for flowers—oh, what a harm!

In the midst of roses, a joke's on the vine,
"Can you smell me?" one flower whispers, divine.
While daisies dance, no care in their sway,
Trading clever quips 'til the end of the day.

The dusk brings laughter; the night makes it swell,
As blossoms confide in an enchanting spell.
In this garden of whimsy, with petals aglow,
Lies a riot of giggles, where secrets bestow.

The Chronicles of a Blooming Soul

In the garden where secrets sway,
A petal whispers, 'I just lost my way!'
A bee buzzes with a cheeky grin,
'You're late to the party, come join in!'

We dance with the wind, we twirl and we spin,
Each color a giggle, each scent a grin.
Don't mind the cats, they plot with a frown,
They think they're kings, but we wear the crown!

At dusk, we gossip in shades of delight,
Sharing our tales under the moonlight.
A rogue snail slides by, we offer a cheer,
'Just take it slow; no need for the fear!'

Oh, laughter binds us in roots intertwined,
In this blooming circus, joy's what we find.
And when morning arrives with a fresh sunny glow,
We'll spill all our stories; come rain or snow!

Language of the Unseen

In the shadow of petals, laughter takes flight,
A worm in a tux dreams of gourmet bites.
'Are you quite sure this is the right path?'
He chuckles and wiggles, 'Let's skip the wrath!'

The daisies gossip, they're full of such flair,
'What's with the roses? Too proud, I declare!'
They chat about blooms that said they could fly,
But wilted too soon, just a glimmering lie!

'Cheer up, dear daisies,' a sunflower beams,
'It's brighter at dawn; let's plot our grand schemes.'
The buzz of the bees dances up in the air,
They'll take back the crown, if they ever could care!

Together we laugh at the antics unheard,
For humor in flora is our secret word.
So let's raise a toast to the fun that we see,
In this vibrant tableau of bloom-light and glee!

The Garden of Unspoken Yearnings

Amidst the greens, a longing is sown,
A daffodil sighs, feeling so alone.
'Where's my match made in sunlight and cheer?'
A crow caws back, 'Good luck with that dear!'

Tulips are blushing, their colors ablaze,
'Time to impress in this pollen-filled maze!'
The violets chuckle, 'We'll keep it light,
Just smile and sway; it'll be alright!'

A glance at the lilies, serene and so bright,
'What do you think of my bold outfit tonight?'
They strut like rock stars, all fancy and free,
While the lilacs nod, 'Just let us be!'

Oh, this is a garden where silly reigns strong,
With mismatched desires, we all sing along.
So let's fling our worries to the soft, gentle breeze,
And laugh at the blooms, oh, come join the tease!

Confidences Among the Blooms

In a cluster of hues, petals gather with glee,
Exchanging their secrets beneath the tall tree.
'What's that you're hiding?' a flower inquired,
'Just last week I tried to get a bee hired!'

The roses all snicker, their thorns held in jest,
'We knew that would fail, just look at your crest!'
But laughter erupts as a ladybug strolls,
'Life's too short for thorns; let's spice up our roles!'

The daisies join in with their innocent charm,
'We'll put on a show; we bring such warm calm!'
As petals unfurl, friendships bloom bright,
With each chuckle shared, we dance through the night.

In whispers we share, with giggles we bind,
The laughter of flora, a sweet life refined.
So gather, dear buds, let our stories ignite,
In this floral saga, everything feels right!

Tales Beneath the Blossom

In the garden where petals play,
Silly secrets dance all day.
A bee's in love with an old shoe,
While worms gossip, saying, "Who knew?"

A snail trips on a sticky leaf,
Laughter echoes, brief but chief.
The daisies giggle, subtly sway,
As polka dots brighten the fray.

A raccoon steals a nutty prize,
While squirrels roll their teasing eyes.
The sun dips low and shares a wink,
And the flowers talk in scented ink.

Under blossoms, stories weave,
Of garden antics you won't believe.
Nature's humor, a blend divine,
Beneath the leaves, all's just fine.

The Language of Fragile Leaves

Leaves chatter in the fluttering breeze,
Whispering jokes with such great ease.
A caterpillar, at tea, draws a laugh,
While ants take turns in a conga path.

A windy gust starts to tease,
Tickling flowers, swaying with ease.
The lilacs plot a grand escape,
While thorns conspire in silly shape.

"Why did the rose blush?" they ask,
"Because it saw the bumblebee's mask!"
Giggles and nods beneath the trees,
All in the language of fragile leaves.

Nature's jesters, a comical crew,
Making humans chuckle, too.
In this garden of whimsy and glee,
The laughter blooms, wild and free.

Shadows of the Garden

In shadows where the petals stretch,
Lurking gnomes begin to sketch.
A pot of jokes beneath the moon,
As crickets play their late-night tune.

Lily pads wear hats with flair,
While frogs croak tunes, a lively air.
Rabbits juggling carrots high,
As owls hoot, "Give it a try!"

When the sun sets, giggles ignite,
Fireflies twinkle, a sparkly sight.
The daisies wear their evening gowns,
While chuckling softly in leafy towns.

In the twilight, laughter grows,
With silly secrets that no one knows.
Where shadows play and mischief sings,
A world of fun that nature brings.

Unraveled Blossoms

Petals tumble in a joyous heap,
As roses giggle, "Oh, not so deep!"
A daffodil trips while trying to dance,
Causing all the tulips to lose their chance.

Breezes tease with ticklish delight,
As sunflowers stretch, reaching for height.
The daisies yell, "Hey, don't you dare!"
And a bee buzzes back, "I'm already there!"

In tangled mess, a bloom takes flight,
A daring jump, oh what a sight!
The garden spins in colorful maze,
Where laughter echoes, oh, what a craze!

With petals scattered, joy unwinds,
In the portrait of nature, humor finds.
Unraveled blossoms, the day's big thrill,
Where giggles thrive, and time stands still.

www.ingramcontent.com/pod-product-compliance
Lightning Source LLC
Chambersburg PA
CBHW071814160426
43209CB00003B/83